Where Is the Great Wall?

D0011209

Where Is the Great Wall?

by Patricia Brennan Demuth

illustrated by Jerry Hoare

Grosset & Dunlap
An Imprint of Penguin Random House

For Joseph Brennan—big heart, deep soul—PBD

GROSSET & DUNLAP
Penguin Young Readers Group
An Imprint of Penguin Random House LLC

If you purchased this book without a cover, you should be aware that this book is stolen property. It was reported as "unsold and destroyed" to the publisher, and neither the author nor the publisher has received any payment for this "stripped book."

Penguin supports copyright. Copyright fuels creativity, encourages diverse voices, promotes free speech, and creates a vibrant culture. Thank you for buying an authorized edition of this book and for complying with copyright laws by not reproducing, scanning, or distributing any part of it in any form without permission. You are supporting writers and allowing Penguin to continue to publish books for every reader.

The publisher does not have any control over and does not assume any responsibility for author or third-party websites or their content.

Text copyright © 2015 by Patricia Brennan. Illustrations copyright © 2015 by Penguin Random House LLC. All rights reserved. Published by Grosset & Dunlap, an imprint of Penguin Random House LLC, 345 Hudson Street, New York, New York 10014. Who HQ™ and all related logos are trademarks owned by Penguin Random House LLC. GROSSET & DUNLAP is a trademark of Penguin Random House LLC. Printed in the USA.

Library of Congress Cataloging-in-Publication Data is available.

ISBN 978-0-448-48358-0   10 9 8 7 6 5 4 3

Contents

BEIJING

THE GREAT WALL

CHINA

Where Is the Great Wall?

More than two thousand years ago, the emperor of China had workers start building a wall. It was a wall like no other on earth—then or now. It has earned its name: the Great Wall. It is the largest structure that humans have ever made!

It is impossible to give its exact length. That's because the Great Wall wasn't built at one time. It's a series of walls constructed over two thousand years, starting in ancient times. Emperors built new walls and linked them to old ones. Some walls decayed and fell apart. But the last Great Wall, built from about 1400 to 1600, still stands. It stretches in an unbroken line four thousand miles across China's northern border. If placed in North America, the main wall would reach from the tip of Florida to the North Pole.

There are also side walls that reach down into China to protect and enclose important places. Altogether, estimates of the Great Wall's length range from about six thousand miles to over ten thousand miles. By any measure, it's huge!

Many compare the Great Wall to a dragon, a symbol of power and strength in China. The head of the wall starts about sixty-six feet offshore, in the Pacific Ocean on China's east coast.

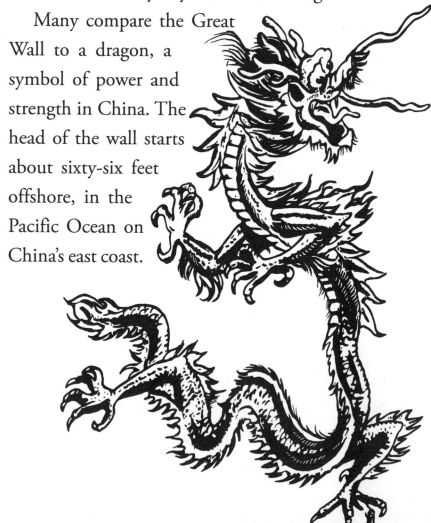

Then it twists and turns through the land—skirting rivers, crossing grasslands and plains, climbing steep mountains, and plunging down cliffs. Finally it ends in the harsh, dry desert on China's western end.

This amazing feat of engineering was *handmade!* There were no machines or power tools to help builders—no forklifts, tractors, drills, or cement mixers. There were just human hands using tools made of stone, iron, and wood. The wall ended up taking a terrible human toll. It is believed that a million Chinese died while building it.

Today the Great Wall awes visitors from all over the world. The story of China itself is told in its bricks, dirt, and stone.

CHAPTER 1
A Reason for Walls

It's been said that China is a land of walls within walls within walls. The ancient Chinese wanted something big and solid to keep out their enemies. So they built walls around their houses, temples, and cities. Wall building is as ancient as China itself. Almost.

Long before the first walls were built, China was a land of nomads. The earliest people roamed from place to place hunting game. Then, about six thousand years ago, the Chinese began to farm. They built homes, tamed animals, and planted crops. Their land was perfect for agriculture. Rich soil filled its plains. Plenty of rain fell. And three giant rivers—the Wei, Yangtze, and Huang He—drained the land.

Farming led to a settled way of life. Fathers worked the same small plots of land all their lives, then passed the land to their sons. Set routines were followed year after year. Farmers planted in the spring and tilled in the summer. In the fall, they stored large amounts of grain to last them through cold winters.

With plenty to eat and safe shelter, the Chinese thrived. Their culture became highly advanced—way ahead of other countries. A written language was developed in China as early as 2200 BC. Learned men started to write China's history on bamboo scrolls and stone. Meanwhile other lands still relied on oral storytelling.

China's Famous Inventions

The entire world has benefited from discoveries made by the Chinese. Here are some of the things China was the first to invent.

SILK

The Chinese found a way to make the soft, fine cloth by harvesting the thread of silkworms. China's oldest silks date back four thousand years.

PORCELAIN

By 1500 BC, Chinese were making early kinds of porcelain—a special kind of pottery made by heating clay at very high temperatures. Jars, plates, and cups made of porcelain became a form of artwork in China. In time, the name "fine china" was given to porcelain, in honor of the country that first made it.

BLAST FURNACE

Metalworkers in China developed a way to melt iron around 500 BC. Their furnaces reached temperatures close to 2,000 degrees Fahrenheit. Europe did not know how to use high-heating methods like this until the Middle Ages.

PAPER

The first paper was made in China in about AD 105 from worn-out fishnet, bamboo bark, and rags.

PRINTING PRESS

Around AD 600, the Chinese were able to print books by using engraved woodblocks. About AD 800, they invented a movable-type press. This was hundreds of years before Gutenberg invented the printing press in Europe in 1453.

GUNPOWDER AND FIREWORKS

Chinese chemists invented gunpowder in AD 800. Before long, they used it to make bombs, rockets, and fireworks.

Artists created beautiful paintings. Craftsmen made statues and containers out of polished bronze. Wise men, such as Confucius, set down their teachings. And women wove soft silk cloth. In time, Chinese silks would be prized around the world.

Life flowed smoothly in ancient China—*except* for enemy attacks from the north. Tribes on horseback roamed the vast grasslands north of China, called the steppe. They were fearsome warriors.

The people of China called the tribes by just one name: barbarians!

Though the barbarians were neighbors with the Chinese, they couldn't have been more different. They lived in round tents called yurts. In place of silks, they wore animal skins. The nomads, who couldn't read or write, drank horse milk and ate cheese, things the Chinese looked down on.

Land on the steppe was much too dry for farming. So the nomads hunted the wild animals that grazed on the grass. They also raised large herds of goats and sheep. When grass grew thin in one place, they packed up their few belongings and moved to the next.

The key to the nomads' way of life was the horse. Indeed, they were the first people in the world to tame horses. Steppe children rode horseback almost as soon as they could walk.

The Steppe

A steppe is any dry, grassy plain. The steppe that stretches across Europe and Asia—from Hungary to China—is so famous that it is often referred to as the Steppe, with a capital *S*. The Steppe is the biggest grassland in the world. It reaches nearly one-fifth of the way around the Earth. In ancient China, the Steppe was mostly north of China. Since the 1400s, it extends into China itself.

The nomads looked with envy at their wealthy neighbors to the south. China had plenty of grain and metal—things that didn't exist on the steppe. The Chinese refused to trade with barbarians. So the nomads stole what they needed instead. In the fall, when the harvest was at its peak, warriors armed with bows and arrows swept down into China. Sometimes small bands of armies raided. Other times, it was just a few hungry horsemen.

Their power lay in surprise attacks—hit and run. Horsemen stormed into farms and villages, shooting with deadly aim while galloping at full speed. They took whatever they could get. Then, in a flash, they disappeared back to the steppe. They left behind ruined villages and many dead.

How could the Chinese protect themselves? Conquering the nomads was impossible. There were too many small tribes. They were scattered all over the steppe and always on the move. The Chinese fell upon a simple answer: they would build walls.

CHAPTER 2
Walls Grow Bigger

The first ancient walls in China were built around 4000 BC. Families built them around their houses and barns. Walls also protected their temples. In time, Chinese cities grew large and put up walls, too. In fact, the Chinese word for *city* means "wall."

City walls enclosed an entire village in a huge square. The tops were wide enough for soldiers to stand guard. Heavy wooden gates were built into opposite sides of a wall. Soldiers guarded them during the day, letting townspeople pass in and out. At night, the gates were closed and locked.

The Chinese made their walls out of dirt. Huge piles of dirt. How could earthen walls stand strong against rain and wind? The secret lay in packing the dirt in thin layers. Each layer was pounded hard—rock hard—before the next layer was added. The Chinese pounded with their feet or simple stone tools. Ramming the earth this way removed all air pockets and kept the wall from sinking later. This method worked so well that the Chinese used it for the next six thousand years!

During the 400s BC, Chinese cities began joining together to form states. Each state was like a small kingdom, covering hundreds of square miles. Ruling over each one was a warlord or king. Every state had different resources. One controlled rich iron mines, another jade. Still other states had forests of bamboo, fertile farmland, or miles of rice paddies.

In time, states began fighting each other for control. Every king wanted to grab others' resources for himself.

To protect their borders, kings started to build longer walls than ever. The biggest city walls had reached twenty miles in length. But state walls stretched up to eight hundred miles long.

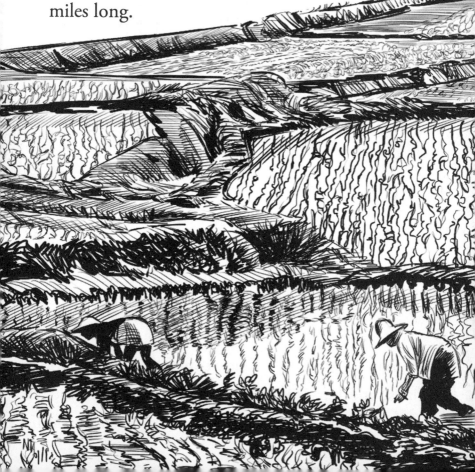

The Iron Age had arrived in China, so building walls was a bit easier. Iron shovels and sharp axes replaced tools made of wood and stone. However, there was nothing new about what went inside the walls. They were still filled with rammed earth.

Fighting peaked between 475 BC and 221 BC. These years became so violent they are now known as the Warring States Period. Armies with tens of thousands of soldiers clashed on battlefields across the land. No longer were barbarians the chief enemy. Now China fought against itself.

Early state battles lasted only a few days. But later on, armies raged against each other for weeks or months at a time. It was all-out war.

Warring States in China

YAN

ZHAO

Gulf of Jili

QI

WEI

Yellow Sea

QIN

HAN

CHU

Huge armies, numbering hundreds of thousands, clashed on battlefields across the land. Battle plans called for attacks on all fronts.

Foot soldiers thrust eighteen-foot pikes and slashed with dagger axes. Warriors on horseback hurled swords and spears. Archers shot from the platforms of charging chariots. Men at mounted crossbows fired arrow after arrow.

In 246 BC, a teenage boy named Zheng took the throne of a state called Qin (chin). By that time, seven states were still standing. Zheng set out to conquer the other six. For the next twenty-five years he waged war. His forces captured ten thousand prisoners in one state—then killed them all.

One by one, states fell to Zheng's military might. Finally, in 221 BC, Zheng crushed the last one. This ruthless man was no longer just King of Qin. He was supreme ruler of all China.

Immediately, he renamed himself Qin Shi Huangdi (chin shee hwong-dee). It means "first emperor of China." Another spelling of *qin* is *ch'in.* So Qin lives on today in the name of the nation he unified: China.

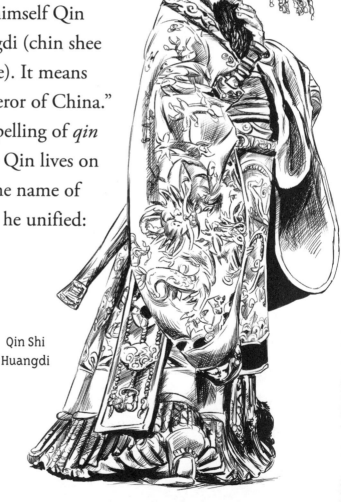

Qin Shi Huangdi

CHAPTER 3
A Ruthless Ruler

China's First Emperor was a man of two extremes. As a leader, he was a genius. Many of his reforms last to this day. As a ruler, he was a tyrant—cruel and unforgiving.

Qin wanted to sweep away China's past. He ordered state walls to be torn down. Kings and warlords were stripped of their lands and weapons. New roads and canals were built to link distant parts of his empire.

For centuries, states had passed different laws, spoken different languages, and paid for goods with different coins. Now the First Emperor commanded that all his subjects do things one way—*his* way.

From then on, there would be just one written language in the land. New coins replaced the old. Traders had to use a single set of weights and measures. The emperor even demanded that carts be made the same width in order to ease road travel.

Most important, he set up a new way to govern the vast empire. Spreading over nearly two million square miles, it was the largest empire in the world—by far. How could the First Emperor organize all the millions of people living in his land? In a brilliant plan, he created the world's first central government. At the bottom were leaders of villages, then leaders of townships, then counties, and so on. Each rank reported to the one above it. At the very top was the emperor. The emperor's far-reaching government turned a group of warring states into one smoothly running empire.

Size of China

The borders of China have shifted through the ages. When the First Emperor united the country, China spread out over one million square miles, from the Pacific Ocean to the edge of the Gobi Desert. Still, it was only about one-third the size of China now. Today, China has more than three and a half million square miles, making it the fourth largest country in the world. With over one billion people, China has the world's largest population.

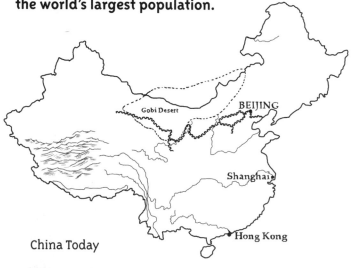

China Today

To stay in control, Emperor Qin cut off all free thought. Scholars, the educated class, had always held high places of honor in China. Kings had often sought their advice. Not the First Emperor! Scholars posed a threat to his power. Qin rounded up 460 leading intellectuals and buried them alive. Next he ordered soldiers to search out all books in the empire and burn them in public bonfires. Only books on medicine and farming were spared.

Scholars tried to save their books by burying them or learning them by heart. If caught, they were killed on the spot.

The emperor's iron fist controlled daily life, too. Citizens needed passes to go anywhere. No one dared to disobey royal orders. They ran the risk of losing a limb, being branded, or—worst—beheaded.

Fear of the emperor spread like a disease through China. "He has all-seeing eyes, the nose of a hornet, the voice of a jackal, and the heart of a wolf," it was reported.

Only one thing lay beyond the emperor's control: barbarian attacks. Regularly, armed nomads still swept down from the north. They had to be stopped. But how? Emperor Qin settled on an age-old solution. He would put up a wall—a wall like none other before it. This one would stretch three *thousand* miles across the northern border!

The First Emperor was about to build the first Great Wall of China.

Confucius

Confucius (551–479 BC) was a Chinese teacher who had an enormous influence on his people. For centuries, men seeking government posts were required to pass a test on his teachings. Confucius taught that people were basically good and that leaders should be kind and just. One of his teachings was the first version of the golden rule: "Do not do to others what you do not wish for yourself." Confucius stressed good behavior—on both the personal and governmental levels. Family loyalty was highly valued, as well. Because of Confucius, every Chinese home kept a shrine to their ancestors.

CHAPTER 4
The First Great Wall Goes Up

Who was going to build the emperor's enormous wall? Nearly every Chinese man who could walk and dig!

The emperor ordered hundreds

of thousands of his subjects to work. Peasants were made to leave their farms. Scholars, who never lifted more than a scroll, were given shovels. Even convicts were hauled from prisons and marched to the wall with chains around their necks. No one went by choice. No one was paid. All were slaves to the empire.

Royal engineers and architects came up with a bold and difficult plan. Beginning at the Yellow Sea in the east, the Great Wall ran three thousand miles across the northern border—all the way to the Gobi Desert. The word *wall* hardly captures

all that went into it. There were also brick towers and outposts—thousands of them! That's where the building began.

Towers had to be made with wood and bricks. To make the bricks, laborers poured mud into wooden molds, then baked them in the sun. The bases of the towers were forty feet square, but the tops were just thirty feet square. Tower walls sloped inward to make them more stable.

Three stories high, the towers served an important role for the army. Weapons were stored inside and troops were housed there. The rooftops were lookout stations as well as places to fight.

During battles, soldiers shot arrows through slits built into the ramparts (low walls) that lined the roof.

Towers were also used to send messages. How was this possible? Through smoke signals! When barbarians were spotted, soldiers raced to build fires in rooftop pits. Smoke billowing into the sky meant *Calling all troops! Come immediately!* A special code alerted other towers to the size of incoming armies. One column of smoke meant that one hundred enemy troops were on the way. Five columns meant *Watch out! One hundred thousand enemy soldiers are attacking!*

When a tower picked up the signal, it too built a fire and passed it along. The Great Wall was one long emergency alarm. And soldiers were running or galloping along the wall to the scene of battle.

Towers were always spaced two arrow shots apart. That way, the enemy was always in firing range from one tower or the next.

Outposts were forts built on the enemy side of the Great Wall. The soldiers who lived there formed the first line of defense. They went forth to meet the enemy before the rest of the Chinese armies arrived.

When laborers finished work on the towers and outposts, they started in on the wall itself. First crews built a frame out of bamboo. It stood as high and wide as the planned wall.

Nearby, supply crews dug up tons of soil. They lugged it to the wall in woven baskets slung across their shoulders. After climbing the frame on ladders, they dumped the dirt over the top.

From there, frame crews took over, spreading and pounding the soil into layers no more than six inches thick. Slowly, layer by layer, the Great Wall rose. When the packed earth finally reached the top of the frame, workers pulled the frame away. Then they moved it down the line to the next spot—and the round of labor began all over again.

Heaps of rubble formed a strong, solid barrier.
When a section of the wall was done, laborers

lined the top with stones. The wall was wide enough for five horsemen to gallop across side by side. In other words, the top of the Great Wall became a paved road!

CHAPTER 5
Downfall

The workers on the Great Wall were treated as slaves. Was it possible to escape? No! The emperor sent three hundred thousand soldiers to stand guard over the workers. Their orders: *Prevent escape. Drive the men hard. Use force if necessary.* Soldiers made sure that crews toiled from sunrise to sunset. During the summer, that meant sixteen-hour workdays in blazing heat. During the winter, the temperature often dropped to freezing. And yet, the work never stopped.

Workers had almost no protection from the weather. They wore whatever clothes they came in, which soon turned into rags. At night they slept in crowded tents or outside on the ground. For food, they got bowls of rice and boiled cabbage.

If supply lines couldn't get through, laborers went hungry for days.

Sickness, severe weather, and exhaustion took their toll. It's believed that seven hundred thousand men died building the first Great Wall. No time was taken to bury the dead. They lay where they fell. The wall became known as "the longest cemetery on earth."

The First Emperor placed little value on other people's lives. And yet death was the one thing that scared him. For years, he searched for a magic potion that would make him live forever. Of course, he never found it. So he ordered seven hundred thousand workers to build him a grand tomb where his body would be placed and could enjoy a happy afterlife. (The emperor buried the tomb laborers alive when their work was finished so they could not disclose the tomb's location.)

The enormous underground tomb covered at least three acres. Standing guard over the emperor's body was a clay army, carefully arranged for battle.

Seven thousand clay soldiers were armed with real weapons—spears, swords, and crossbows. All stood as big as life. Yet no two looked alike. Chinese artists crafted the soldiers from terracotta, a reddish-brown clay. Some knelt at crossbows. Some were placed in chariots pulled by life-size horses.

Before his tomb could be finished, the First Emperor suddenly died at age forty-nine. The year was 210 BC. No one knows for sure if the hated ruler was killed or died of natural causes.

Word of his death flew quickly through

the empire. Uprisings broke out, joined by thousands of peasants. Just four years after Qin died, his dynasty was overthrown. (A dynasty is a family that stays in control of an empire.) It had lasted only fifteen years.

Yet the First Emperor's achievements lived on. The Chinese empire lasted into the twentieth century. And Qin's basic wall plan was used by subsequent emperors for two thousand years!

The First Emperor's Tomb

The secret of the emperor's tomb was kept for more than two thousand years. Then in 1974, near the city of Xian (SHEE-ahn), some peasants were drilling a well. They dug up part of one of the terra-cotta soldiers. That was how the tomb was discovered. Soon restoration of the clay army began, and it

continues today. More than a million people from around the globe visit Xian to see the soldiers.

Much of the tomb has yet to be unearthed. The Chinese fear that air may destroy the priceless treasures within. Ancient texts disclose that the tomb contains a model of the Chinese empire. Gems and pearls on the wooden roof shine like the sun, moon, and stars. Models of China's great rivers—made of liquid mercury—flow through the tiny kingdom. Recent findings suggest that the burial ground is much larger than anyone had thought—maybe twenty square miles!

CHAPTER 6
Peace Along the Wall

China had always closed itself off from the outside world. But that started to change in 206 BC when the Han dynasty took the throne. Lasting 426 years, the rule of the Hans became a remarkable time in Chinese history. Han emperors opened China's gates wide and invited in other nations. The Great Wall took on a brand-new role—a peacetime role.

The Chinese had suffered terribly under the heartless rule of the First Emperor. So the first goal of the Han dynasty was to restore peace and harmony to their people. Scholars were treated with honor again. Buried books were dug up. Soon the arts and learning thrived. Scientists invented paper, the first in the world. Writing on

bamboo scrolls or stones was no longer necessary.

Han rulers had little to do with the Great Wall at first. The Chinese people were fed up with the project. But in time, the steppe nomads began raiding again.

In 141 BC, a Han emperor named Wudi took action. Chinese troops launched an all-out attack against tribes living near their border. The barbarians were driven farther back into the steppe. Meanwhile Wudi sent workers to repair the Great Wall and keep raiders from returning.

Emperor Wudi also built three hundred miles of new wall. Planning it was easy. He simply followed the First Emperor's design— walls of packed earth, towers, and outposts.

The surprise was *where* the new wall went up. It was built in the endless, empty wasteland of the Gobi Desert. A long chain of towers was also added beyond the wall's end. The last tower reached the very edge of China's western border.

Beyond the border lay routes to the Western worlds of Europe, Asia, and Africa.

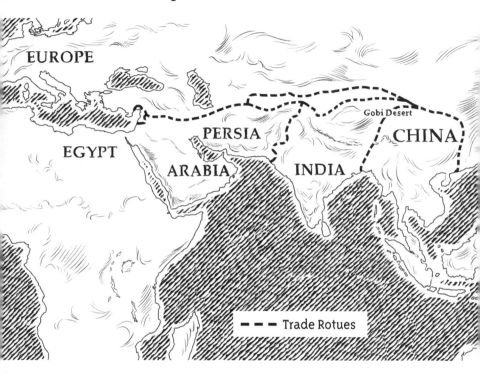

Why did Wudi extend the Great Wall into this forbidding desert? He had decided to open up trade with the West and use the wall to safeguard travelers. The Chinese had treasures found no place else in the world. Other nations were eager to buy China's teas, spices, porcelain, paper, jade, and—most prized of all—silk.

By then, the Chinese had already been making silk for three thousand years. Other nations didn't know how to make the beautiful, shimmering cloth. And the Chinese were not about to tell them. If other nations wanted silk, they had to travel all the way to China to get it. A trade route to China took form that would prosper for centuries. It became known as the Silk Road.

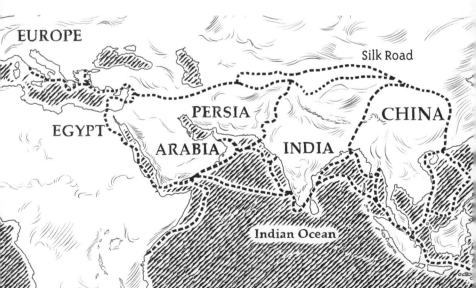

EUROPE

Silk Road

PERSIA

CHINA

EGYPT

ARABIA

INDIA

Indian Ocean

Making Silk

Making lovely silks starts with the work of the humble silkworm. To make its cocoon, a silkworm spins a thin, strong line of silk. It can be three thousand feet long!

Around 2000 BC, the Chinese discovered how to unravel the thread and turn it into cloth. They first loosen and unwind the threads from a silkworm's cocoon. Next, they combine the fibers to make thread. Finally, the threads are woven into cloth on wooden looms.

Silks played an important role in China's economy for thousands of years. Kings and nobles from other lands were willing to pay high prices for the fine, soft cloth. For thousands of years, China closely guarded its silk-making secret from outsiders. Giving away the secret was a crime punished by death.

The Silk Road was not actually a road. It was the name given to a network of trade routes that led to China. The start-off points were distant lands in Asia and Europe, as much as four thousand miles away. All routes came together at the farthest tower of the Great Wall.

From there, traders traveled along the wall in long camel caravans. Going through the Gobi Desert put their lives at risk. Water was nowhere in sight. Sunlight baked down nonstop. Whipping winds blew the desert into towering mountains of sand. Without camels—the great beasts of desert travel—traders could not survive. Traders ended their journeys at different points. Some braved the long journey all the way to China's east coast.

Beasts of the Desert

The huge and homely camel was the hero of the Silk Road. It was perfectly suited for desert travel. Camels can go for a week without a drink of water. They survive by eating tough desert plants. Their splayed hoofs keep them from sinking in the hot sands. All the while, they can bear up to nine hundred pounds on their strong, humped backs.

Thousands of soldiers at the Great Wall protected traders from bandits. Their jobs were something like those of today's police or border guards. Soldiers checked passes at the gates, enforced the rules, and captured outlaws.

Rarely did soldiers need to fight. Peace reigned along the Great Wall. Even the steppe nomads became friendly trading partners with the Chinese. Still, peace along the wall would not last forever.

CHAPTER 7
Breaking into China

For a thousand years after the Han, dynasties came and went. Few emperors kept up repairs on the Great Wall. After centuries of neglect, much of the wall crumbled into dust.

Off and on, raiders from the north still thundered over the border. Though they spread ruin, the Chinese never had feared the nomads taking over their nation. After all, China was big, rich, and strong. The steppe tribes were small and scattered far apart. Often the tribes warred against one another. Without unity, they posed no real threat to China.

That all changed in the 1200s. A strong and fearsome warrior rose up on the steppe from the Mongol tribe. His name was Genghis (JING-gis) Khan, which means "ruler of all men." As a young man, Genghis gathered a powerful army and conquered enemy tribes of his people. Then he worked to unite the many other tribes. Warriors from the far reaches of the steppe galloped forth to join his forces and fight under his banner. The Mongol army swelled to 130,000 horsemen.

With his homeland united, Genghis set out to conquer the known world. The Mongols fought

Genghis Khan

their way through Asia and into Europe. Cities fell to the mighty warriors; then entire countries. Within decades, the Mongols captured the biggest empire the world has ever known!

Genghis hungered to take over China most of all. China was the biggest prize—and the hardest to capture.

In 1211, Genghis stormed over the old wall and took control of northern China. Then his forces pushed on south. But there he ran into problems. The dense forests tripped up the Mongols' horses. And China's huge cities, defended by massive armies, refused to fall. Genghis died in 1227 without seeing his dream to rule China come true.

A later ruler of the Mongols, Kublai Khan, was not about to give up the cause. Kublai was the grandson of Genghis. He matched his grandfather's skill and fury in warfare. In 1279, Kublai's warriors forced their way into the Chinese capital and killed the emperor.

Kublai Khan

For the Chinese, it was their worst nightmare! Not only were the barbarians inside their borders, they ruled their nation. Ten million Chinese had fallen under Mongol control.

However, once the bloodshed was over, Kublai led China wisely. He kept the well-running government layers in place. Still, the top levels were now filled by Mongols, not Chinese. Foreigners were also allowed to work for the royal court. This had been unheard of before! Among them was the Italian adventurer Marco Polo, whose stories of Chinese wonders spread through Europe.

Marco Polo

Marco Polo (1254–1324) traveled to China with his father and uncle when he was just seventeen years old. They were merchants and hoped to find riches to sell in China. Kublai Khan, the Mongol ruler of China, immediately took a liking to Marco and hired him to work for his court. After learning the languages of both the Chinese and Mongols, Marco served as a messenger for Kublai. He saw marvels that no one from Europe had ever seen before. After seventeen years, Marco Polo returned home. His firsthand accounts of China helped to kick-start a new age of exploration in Europe. Some say his tales inspired the travels of Christopher Columbus, which led to the discovery of the New World.

Kublai moved his capital to Beijing (bay-jing) in northern China. (Beijing remains the capital today.) A grand walled palace was built for him in the middle of the city. Kublai and his court lived there in splendor.

Even though daily life hadn't changed much, the Chinese hated being ruled by outsiders. The Mongols spoke a different language and had different customs. To the Chinese, they were still barbarians. When Kublai Khan died in 1294, many saw their chance to take their country back.

CHAPTER 8
The Glory Years

Genghis Khan and his grandson Kublai were both powerful leaders. But weaker rulers followed them. The Chinese took this chance to revolt. In 1368, an angry peasant uprising succeeded in overthrowing the Mongols and chasing them back to the steppe. The Ming dynasty was founded. For almost three hundred years, Ming emperors would rule China and bring the Great Wall into its years of glory.

The Mongols had let the remains of the first Great Wall fall away into a heap of dirt. Why not? They controlled the land on both sides of the wall anyway. So the Ming decided to start from scratch and build a Great Wall of their own. The capital city, Beijing, now lay just a dozen miles from the

steppe. It was much too close to the enemy for comfort.

The project of building a new wall passed from one Ming emperor to the next. Each one followed the basic plan set down by the First Emperor and then the Han rulers. The insides were still rammed dirt. Towers still linked miles of wall. But the Ming Wall was bigger, better, and more beautiful. Brick and stone lined its walls and base. Nearly all of the Great Wall that tourists see today was built by the Ming emperors.

Anyone could build a dirt wall. But walls of brick and stone required special skills. Stonecutters and brick masons were hired—hundreds of thousands of them.

The base was made from giant slabs of granite—one of the hardest stones on earth. Working at quarries, skilled stonecutters chipped away at the rock using just hammers and chisels.

The blocks had to be smooth in order to fit closely together. It was painstaking work. The biggest granite blocks weighed two tons and stood two stories high!

Then came the backbreaking job of hauling the granite to the wall site. One way was loading the massive stone onto carts, using pulleys and rollers. It took hundreds of mules to lug the carts to the wall.

Once the base was put in place, brick masons set to work. They built two brick walls on top of the stone, thirty feet high and twenty-five feet apart. These walls formed the framework of

the Ming Wall. Dirt and rubble was packed and pounded inside.

Countless clay bricks went into the wall. Expert masons baked them in kilns—small ovens shaped like beehives. Holes in the top let out smoke. The bricks had to bake for hours in very hot fires. Once the blazes died, they were cooled  inside the kilns for days before being removed.

Technology had advanced since the first walls were built. New inventions made some jobs easier. For instance, with a wheelbarrow, a worker could carry loads uphill with much less difficulty. Ropes and pulleys now raised and lowered baskets of supplies. Workers filled the baskets at the bottom of the wall. Then they cranked them up to the top where they were emptied. When the baskets were lowered to the ground, they were filled again. Pulley systems were also rigged over mountain ravines. Baskets loaded with supplies swung in the air until they reached the other side.

Drains

Ming engineers added drains to the Great Wall. That way, rainwater poured out of spouts instead of seeping into bricks and causing cracks. Without these pipes, the Great Wall would not still be standing today.

Despite these advances, human hands and backs still bore the brunt of the labor. "Workers paid dearly in sweat and blood," said historian Luo Zewen.

By far the hardest places to build the wall were over sheer, steep mountain cliffs. The Ming Wall followed the natural line of the peaks. It seemed as if the wall grew straight out of the mountains. It wasn't that easy! Workers hacked through solid rock to dig pits in which stone and bricks were laid.

Getting heavy supplies up towering peaks was also hard. Human chains, sometimes miles long, passed loads of brick, rock, and dirt from one person to the next. Pack animals helped, too. Goats with bags of bricks tied to their horns labored up mountainsides.

The Ming emperors weren't satisfied with a Wall that was strong and towering. It had to be beautiful, too. Bricks were laid in perfect patterns. Carved arches covered gates. Towers were sometimes as ornate as temples. Artwork like this served no military purpose at all. It existed just to please the fine taste of the Ming empire.

The Last Fort

Far west in the Gobi Desert, the Ming built a famous fort named Jiayuguan (jah-yoo-gwan). They called it the "First and Greatest Pass Under Heaven." Here's where the Great Wall ends. Its design is a masterpiece, and no enemy ever captured it. The stronghold is actually a fort within a fort, covering eight acres. A moat surrounds the inner and outer cities. Anyone who enters the fort must make their way through a puzzling maze of gates, towers, and walls. All these are designed to confuse attackers.

CHAPTER 9
Life at the Wall

"A wall is only as strong as the men who guard it," Genghis Khan once said. The Ming Wall was manned by one million soldiers. Why were so many needed? The Mongols wanted to get China back.

Soldiers spent their entire lives at the towers of the wall. They lived nearby with their families— not in forts but on their own small farms. These farmer-soldiers, as they were called, raised all the food they needed to eat.

Forts on both sides of the wall were filled with soldiers, too. On the enemy side of the wall, soldiers lived in outposts, just as they'd done in the time of the First Emperors. On the Chinese side, enormous forts housed up to a thousand royal troops. Highly trained, the Chinese army stood ever ready for battle.

At night, tower guards spread sand on the north side of the wall. In the morning, they checked it for footprints. Trusted dogs, which lived at the towers, went along to sniff for signs of the enemy.

Firepower made warfare more deadly than ever. Chinese soldiers still rained down arrows at the enemy, firing from slits built into ramparts on the wall. But beginning in the 1100s, they also used cannon power. Mongol armies fought back

just as hard. Using catapults, they hurled boulders that smashed at the wall or crashed down on soldiers at the top.

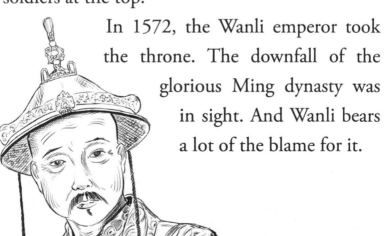

In 1572, the Wanli emperor took the throne. The downfall of the glorious Ming dynasty was in sight. And Wanli bears a lot of the blame for it.

Wanli

The emperor lived in the world's largest palace in the heart of the capital city, Beijing. The palace was large enough to be called a city: the Forbidden City. It was called "forbidden" because only the emperor and his court were allowed to enter. Peasants had to keep out.

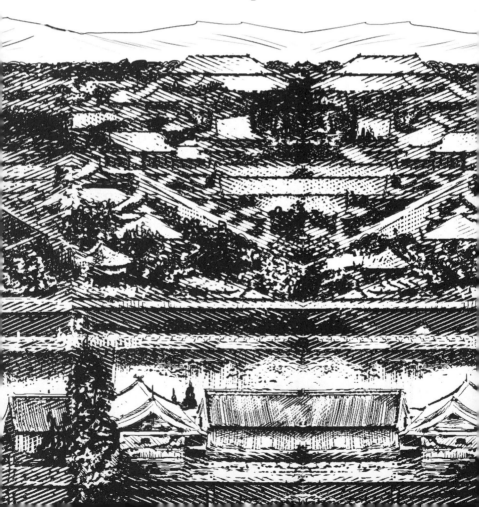

Spread out over 185 acres of land, the Forbidden City contained about a thousand buildings and nine thousand rooms! All of it was dazzling! Royal crimson colored the walls. Stairs were made of marble, and roof tiles were golden. The emperor lived there in total luxury—along with tens of thousands of servants and advisers. The royal court waited on his every whim. One of the emperor's robes took thirteen years to make!

At first the Ming empire continued to thrive under Wanli. But then the emperor grew tired of his royal duties. For the last twenty years of his rule, the emperor refused to meet with his officials. Reports went unread. Government leaders who died were not replaced. Every day, officials arrived for their royal meeting and bowed to the emperor's throne—just an empty chair!

During this decline, soldiers at the Great Wall went unpaid. Soon, they began to wander away from their jobs. It was a bad time for the Chinese to let down their guard. A new power—the Manchu tribe—was gathering on the steppe.

Meanwhile, Chinese peasants rose up in revolt. They were angry about paying higher and higher taxes to support a richer and richer royal lifestyle. The court dressed in silk and feasted at every meal. The emperor himself grew so obese he couldn't stand up without aid. Meanwhile, peasant families starved.

Chinese rebels broke into the Forbidden City in 1644, killing the emperor. But the Ming dynasty had not come to its final end—not quite yet. A massive force of Manchu soldiers had gathered at the Great Wall. The desperate Ming court sent word seeking their help in exchange for favors.

It was a fateful moment in Chinese history. The Manchu agreed to the plea; a Chinese general opened the gate. For centuries, the Chinese had fought off the barbarians at the Great Wall. Now the Manchu army simply walked through with their horses!

From there, Manchu soldiers tore into Beijing and overthrew the rebels. Then all bets were off. The Manchu took power for themselves. Manchurians would rule China for nearly three hundred years, all the way into the 1900s.

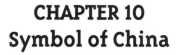

CHAPTER 10
Symbol of China

When the Ming Dynasty ended in 1644, so did the glory days of the Great Wall. Building came to a complete stop, never to be resumed. For centuries, towers and outposts remained empty.

Wind, rain, and snow ate away at the stone and brick. In the desert, towering sand dunes buried big sections of the wall. Yet, mile after mile of the Great Wall still stood proudly over China's landscape.

People's Republic of China

Emperors ruled China from 221 BC, when the First Emperor united the country, until 1912. That year the last dynasty fell. China became a republic ruled by a president. Unrest followed for several years. Then, in 1949, the Communist Party took control. They created the People's Republic of China, and they continue to rule to this day. China has a one-party system: only the Chinese Communist Party is allowed to govern. In 2013, Xi Jinping (SHEE jin-PING) took over as head of the party and supreme leader of China.

Then, in the 1960s, the Great Wall suffered its worst blow. This time nature was not to blame. China had entered a period in its history known as the Cultural Revolution. The Communist Party, which had governed China since 1949, wanted to erase all ties with the past. Rare books were burned. Priceless bronze artworks were melted down for scrap metal. Men and women of higher learning were tortured and killed.

The Chinese people had suffered this kind of harsh treatment from the First Emperor two thousand years earlier. There was a large difference, however. The First Emperor *built* the first Great Wall. The leaders behind the Cultural Revolution wanted to *tear* the wall down.

Bulldozers smashed down hundreds of miles of the Wall to make way for modern buildings and freeways. Dynamite exploded stones and bricks that had been in place over five hundred years.

By 1984, a new Communist government had taken charge under Deng Xiaoping (dung shouping). Almost overnight, the fate of the Great Wall took a U-turn. "Let us love our country and restore our Great Wall," said Xiaoping. A renewed sense of pride for the country's remarkable history began to grow in China. And the Great Wall won a new place in peoples' hearts. A large-scale project to repair and restore the wall was begun. It continues to this day.

Deng Xiaoping

The West had known almost nothing about the Great Wall for a long time. Then in 1972, President Richard Nixon became the first US president to visit China. Broadcasts of Nixon standing on the Great Wall brought the landmark to the world's attention.

So did a gift from the Chinese to the United Nations in New York City. In 1974, China presented the United Nations with a tapestry that showcased the majesty of the Great Wall. It weighed six hundred pounds and measured thirty-two feet long. The tapestry now hangs in the delegates' lounge, proudly declaring the wall as the symbol of China.

President Nixon's Visit

US President Richard Nixon made history when he visited China in 1972. For twenty years, China had closed off its borders to almost all visitors.

The Cultural Revolution was at its height, and the government was destroying miles of the Great Wall when Nixon came. Still, the Communist leader, Chairman Mao Zedong, took Nixon there. Mao quoted an old Chinese saying, "You're not a man until you've climbed to the top." Nixon's visit sparked worldwide interest in the Great Wall.

Today, ten million people visit it every year. They stand in wonder at its size and beauty. They marvel at its engineering. They pay tribute to the people of China—one of the oldest civilizations on earth.

Timeline of the Great Wall

4000 BC	The earliest Chinese people settle in homes and begin farming
2200 BC	The Chinese develop a written language
2000 BC	The earliest silks are woven
1500 BC	The first porcelain is fired
551 BC	The great teacher Confucius is born
500 BC	Chinese melt iron in an early form of blast furnaces
400s BC	Chinese cities group together in states
475 BC	The Warring States Period begins, lasting until 221 BC
221 BC	Qin Shi Huangdi, the First Emperor, begins work on the first Great Wall
206 BC	The Han dynasty takes the throne and rules until AD 220
141 BC	Han emperor Wudi adds three hundred miles to the first Great Wall to safeguard traders on the Silk Road
105 BC	The Chinese invent paper
AD 800	The Chinese invent a movable-type press
1211	Genghis Khan leads the Mongols into China
1279	Under Kublai Khan, the Mongols capture China
1368	The Ming dynasty, which builds the Great Wall seen today, is founded
1644	The Manchu overthrow the Ming dynasty and control China into the twentieth century
1974	The terra-cotta army is discovered
1984	The Communist government begins restoring the Great Wall
1987	UNESCO names the Great Wall a World Heritage Site

Timeline of the World

People of the Eurasian steppe tame the horse	3500 BC
Greek poet Homer completes the *Iliad* and the *Odyssey*	ca. 700 BC
The Romans begin writing in Latin	300s BC
The fall of the ancient Rome	AD 476
Italian adventurer Marco Polo arrives in China	1271
Incas in the Andes feed their millions through terrace farming	1400s
German Johannes Gutenberg invents the printing press	1440
Bartholomew Diaz sails around the southern tip of Africa	1488
Christopher Columbus arrives in the New World	1492
Italian astronomer Galileo, using his new telescope, discovers Jupiter's four largest moons	1610
US President Richard Nixon visits China and raises worldwide interest in the Great Wall	1972

Bibliography

*Books for young readers

*Coupe, Robert. *The Great Wall of China.* New York: Rosen
Publishing Group, 2013.

*DuTemple, Lesley A. *The Great Wall of China.* Minneapolis:
Lerner Publications, 2003.

Gernet, Jacques. *A History of Chinese Civilization.* New York:
Cambridge University Press, 1982.

*Mann, Elizabeth. *The Great Wall.* New York: Mikaya Press, 1997.

*McNeese, Tim. *The Great Wall of China.* San Diego: Lucent
Books, 1997.

Zewen, Luo, Dai Wenbao, Dick Wilson, J. P. Drege, and H. Delahaye.
The Great Wall. New York: McGraw-Hill, 1981.

Periodicals and DVDs

China Revealed: The Great Wall. Discovery Channel Video, 2006.

Secrets of the Forbidden City. Directed by Mark Lewis. With
Jacqueline Chow, Kee Thuan Chye, Tony Quek, Anthony
Brandon Wong. A&E Television Networks: History, 2008. Film.

Wild China. Narrated by Bernard Hill. Produced by Phil Chapman
BBC Earth, 2008. TV series.

RUSSIA

KAZAKHSTAN

MONGOL

URUMQI

RGYZSTAN

HIMALAYAS

TSANGPO-BRAHMAPUTRA RIVER

MEKONG RIVER

NU JIANG RIVER

NEPAL

BHUTAN

LIJIANG

INDIA

BANGLADESH

MYANMAR (BURMA)

LAOS

Map illustration by Abi Daker. © Penguin Group (USA) LLC.
Photo © Thinkstock, photographed by MilaSemenova